Investing

Comprehensive Tutorial For Novice Investors On
Maximizing Returns From Real Estate Foreclosures

*(Strategies For Generating Profit Through Foreclosure
Short Sales And Investments In Foreclosed Properties)*

Jared Charette

TABLE OF CONTENT

Can One Sustain A Livelihood Solely Through Passive Income Derived From Dividends?

You may be pondering the potential value of allocating your time towards investing in stock dividends. Historically, these dividends have been regarded as a means of mitigating exposure to uncertainties in the stock market. Frankly speaking, dividends provide a notable avenue to enhance one's income. If one chooses to sustain oneself solely through stock dividends, it is imperative to comprehend the considerable challenges that lie ahead. The accumulation of passive income from such stocks occurs gradually. Should the need arise for the utilization of this particular approach to generate income, it is highly advisable to commence at the earliest feasible opportunity, as the investment in question can also serve the purpose of a retirement fund.

Due to the gradual nature of stock dividend investments, one cannot immediately rely on them as a source of income upon making the investment. It is a process that evolves gradually. With a well-developed strategy and meticulous planning, it is indeed feasible to accomplish this objective within a span of several years. An essential element of dividend investing entails focusing on stocks with a propensity for growth. These are stocks that experience an annual growth in the dividend payout. This indicates that your passive income will continue to grow without any additional contributions to your investment capital.

Dividends are distributed solely to shareholders in acknowledgment of their membership in a specific corporation. There is no requirement for you to engage in any activities other than conducting research on stocks and carefully choosing a suitable company. The investment you make operates in your favor. When contrasting this approach with other methods of generating passive income, it is evident that dividends considerably simplify the process of investing and earning. The majority of the alternative sources of income are not entirely passive in nature, as they require a considerable amount of effort to generate earnings.

However, there is a downside. In order to achieve a substantial income from dividend stocks, it is imperative to possess a respectable amount of capital. To achieve absolute financial liberation from this venture, one must be prepared to make considerable sacrifices. Based on the preceding example, it is evident that the acquisition of 100 shares of stock from Company B results in an annual dividend of $500. If the price per share is $100, it would require a total investment of $10,000. Assuming your objective is to attain an annual passive income of $50,000, it would be necessary to acquire a total of 10,000 shares in the company. The investment capital totals $1,000,000. This is essentially what you require, excluding additional factors such as fluctuations in stock prices and taxation.

Investing a million dollars in such a trade amounts to a significant sum, however, the potential returns are exceedingly profitable. For the majority of investors, attaining such a substantial sum of money is a formidable task that could require several years of effort. For this very rationale, a majority of investors commence their investment journey by allocating their funds to growth stocks. Notwithstanding the inherent risks, the aforementioned investments also exhibit the highest rates of return. After acquiring a sufficient amount of profit from these stocks, it would be advisable to contemplate substituting them with dividend stocks. In the initial stages of your foray into the stock market, you may consider exploring alternative forms of stock, while concurrently incorporating dividend stocks into your growing investment portfolio.

Dividend-bearing equities possess diverse attributes that distinguish them from alternative forms of stock investments. Presented here are a few examples.

Dividend stocks can indicate either a single enterprise or a group of companies. These aid in the identification of optimal investment opportunities as companies lacking dividend payments often become ineligible for consideration within this classification.

The determination of a corporation to distribute dividends is typically achieved through the consensus of multiple stakeholders. Given that this determination emanates from a collective body, comprising primarily the board and management team, you maintain a steadfast conviction that the disbursement of your dividends shall duly ensue, notwithstanding any underperformance of the company's stock valuation.

A set of regulations is established for each stock market to oversee the disbursement of dividends. Despite the fact that the decision to distribute dividends lies with the management of a company, these policies serve to ensure that shareholders receive their entitled payments as intended.

Typically, dividends are only extended to shareholders by well-established corporations in the majority of instances. Acquiring shares from these companies guarantees the safety and protection of your investment. Many small companies consistently face challenges when it comes to distributing dividends due to their ongoing pursuit of operational expansion. Large corporations are recognized for their consistent and forecastable cash flows. Their formidable presence in the stock market guarantees a sufficient level of profitability that can simultaneously support the company's operations and provide dividends to its shareholders.

In general, dividend stocks tend to exhibit lower volatility than other types of stocks. This phenomenon can be attributed to the relatively gradual price fluctuations of said stocks, which can be ascribed to the substantial investor base.

In addition to offering potential financial gains, investing in dividend stocks confers certain tax benefits. Similar to conventional stocks, the gains obtained from your stock investments are subject to taxation solely upon the sale of said investments. The uppermost tax rate applicable to dividends is a mere 15%. This quantity appears significantly diminished in relation to alternative investment options, such as bonds. It additionally exhibits a lower magnitude in comparison to all other revenue streams.

Diversification

Diversification serves as a crucial tactic employed by long-term investors. This advice is in alignment with the time-honored wisdom of diversifying your investments or resources. Undoubtedly, it remains sound counsel even in contemporary times.

Let us assume that you possess shares in the FAANGs, an informal designation employed within financial markets to refer to the prominent technology corporations. Broadly speaking, this encompasses Facebook, Apple, Amazon, Netflix, and Google. Nevertheless, this encompasses various other companies including Twitter and SNAP, among others.

Now, in the event that Congress were to opt for an investigation into the FAANG companies concerning matters of privacy or even potential monopolistic practices. Indeed, that is transpiring even as I compose this statement. Should you have allocated your entire investment portfolio to the five companies forming this group, which is facing mounting scrutiny from Congress, the U.S. government, and notably the European Union, it is conceivable that you would encounter unfavorable investment outcomes.

As an alternative illustration, consider the scenario in which you exclusively allocated your investments in enterprises associated with the healthcare industry. In the event that either Bernie Sanders or Elizabeth Warren emerges victorious in the Presidential election and concurrently secures a Congress under Democratic control... It is possible that they may enact a Medicare for All legislation that would result in the complete elimination of private health insurance. From a pragmatic standpoint, it is worth considering that all of the companies in which you have financial stakes may potentially be compelled to explore alternative avenues and could additionally face the prospect of insolvency. At a minimum, if such a bill were to be enacted, it is highly likely that their stock prices would significantly decline, thereby resulting in a considerable negative impact on your investments.

These illustrations demonstrate that concentrating investments in a small number of companies, particularly within the same sector, is not a prudent investment approach. While the instance of governmental intervention was employed as an illustrative example, it should be acknowledged that numerous factors possess the potential to exert influence on individual firms or the respective industries they operate in. Therefore, it encompasses not only significant government measures.

In summary, it is not advisable to concentrate all of one's investments solely in a few healthcare companies, or exclusively in Google and Amazon. However, it is possible to achieve portfolio balance by diversifying investments across various sectors and multiple companies. This approach serves to safeguard against the aforementioned concerns outlined earlier.

Frequently, an interconnected yet distinct industry can experience advantages in situations where another industry is encountering challenges. In the event that oil companies encounter unforeseen challenges, natural gas or solar energy could potentially experience a surge in popularity. Individuals will actively search for alternative avenues to allocate their funds in the event that a particular sector encounters difficulties.

However, even in this context, the darker facets of human nature can manifest themselves. Individuals often develop preferential attitudes towards specific companies. As one delves into the analysis of companies' financial records and gains familiarity with their products and prospective strategies, it is likely that one will develop a strong affinity for certain firms. The peril associated with this situation is an excessive concentration of capital in a solitary investment. This serves as an additional illustration of the diverse range of ways in which emotions can impact investment decisions, and it is not invariably to one's advantage. Undoubtedly, it is permissible to experience enthusiasm for a particular corporation, and allocating investments towards it could be deemed a prudent decision. However, it would have been advisable to establish guidelines regarding the allocation of investment funds to individual companies. And it is imperative that you do not surpass that guideline.

We retain the ability to retrospectively assess the historical performance of companies, yet the prospective performance of said companies remains uncertain. There are several variables that will impact the company's performance over time. Similarly, accurately determining when a trend will reverse or identifying companies that will thrive in the next decade or two is a challenge. Therefore, it is advisable to diversify your investments across a portfolio of different companies. We have limited capacity to influence the outcome in our favor, yet we lack control over the ultimate course of events.

This leads us to the primary advantage that you will reap from establishing a diversified portfolio. We have conducted a thorough examination of dividend stocks and have made estimations regarding the potential income they can generate for you. Nonetheless, the prosperity of a corporation can decline unexpectedly. Take into account Abbvie, a company that we have consistently referred to as a favorable investment opportunity. At present, it represents a favorable investment opportunity, given its substantial dividend payout and commendable track record.

However, should our current government, which exhibits a growing inclination towards left-wing ideologies and populism, implement policies such as universal healthcare (Medicare for all) or the imposition of controls on prescription drug prices, what implications might this have? Such circumstances could potentially adversely impact the future prospects of a pharmaceutical company such as Abbvie. In the event that both of these circumstances transpire, there exists the potential for a significant downturn in their fortunes, ultimately leading to potential constraints on their ability to uphold their dividend disbursements.

In the event that you had allocated all of your financial resources into AbbVie, it is plausible to anticipate potential difficulties arising in the future. In addition to the potential reduction in dividend payments, it is conceivable that the share price could experience a significant decrease. This would imply that in the event of selling your shares to exit and pursue a more favorable investment, you could potentially incur a significantly diminished capital compared to your initial investment.

The objective of diversification is as follows for the dividend-focused investor. Having a robust and well-diversified investment portfolio ensures that your income stream is not contingent on the performance of a single stock. In the event that Abbvie constitutes a mere 5-10% of your entire investment portfolio, as opposed to constituting 100% or even 50%, should it encounter adverse circumstances in the future, you will still have the capacity to endure, derive gains, and progress.

It is imperative to bear in mind that as a dividend investor, you hold a vested interest in two primary factors. These constitute the financial resources you utilized for the acquisition of the shares, along with the stability or growth of the dividend disbursements. Diversification helps with both. To put it differently, the preservation of your capital can be ensured through the cultivation of a varied portfolio. By possessing a collection of 10 or 20 stocks, the possibility of unfavorable outcomes for all holdings is reduced. It is highly probable that, in the long run, if you have made prudent choices, only a minor proportion of your stocks will exhibit unfavorable performance. This implies that through the implementation of a well-diversified portfolio, one can effectively safeguard their invested capital.

Ultimately, certain stocks are poised to experience a decline. Diversification is imperative for enhancing the security of your investments and reducing the potential for losses. By including a variety of stocks in your portfolio, any decline in certain holdings can be offset by the gains made in others. The losses will be mitigated to minimize their impact on you through an averaging process. Indeed, in certain instances, one can still be at an advantageous position, as there is a potential for substantial gains on select investment endeavors.

Now we must contemplate the implications of diversification, particularly in the context of dividend investing. People typically discuss diversification using broad, general language. For an imaginary typical investor, diversification would entail allocating investments across a combination of aggressive growth stocks, value stocks, bonds, and cash.

Nevertheless, as shareholders focused on dividend investments, we shall approach the matter from a different perspective. Therefore, our intention is not to safeguard against the stock market itself, but rather to shield ourselves from any potential difficulties that may befall certain individual stocks.

We have identified three distinct forms in which diversification can be pursued. Our primary objective is to diversify our investments across a considerable number of companies, ensuring that none hold undue influence over the performance of our portfolio. As a minimum requirement, it is advisable to allocate investments to at least ten companies. A score of twenty is significantly superior, albeit requiring additional effort. An excess of information may prove overwhelming once the quantity surpasses twenty. Therefore, it is advisable to select a maximum of twenty-five companies.

Now, you are faced with the inquiry of determining the appropriate allocation for each company. It is advisable to distribute your investments in a reasonably equitable manner. It is not advisable to allocate 50% or even 25% of your funds to a singular company.

There are numerous companies that appear to be highly favorable options for investment, given the current circumstances. That assertion may indeed remain valid in the context of the long-term, yet it is imperative to reiterate that the uncertainty surrounding future outcomes remains a prevailing factor in the long-term scenario. A firm such as Boeing or Disney could potentially be deemed a sound investment not only presently, but also over the course of the next three decades. We currently lack any discernment regarding the events that will transpire in the interim. Furthermore, it is important to note that markets have the potential to undergo significant upheaval in their entirety. Enterprises that formerly enjoyed commanding market positions can eventually become mere remnants of their former selves.

Therefore, it is advisable to avoid the risk associated with concentrating a significant portion of your investment capital in a single company. A plethora of companies are available on the stock market, offering dividend payouts. Therefore, allocating your investments among a range of 10 to 20 reputable companies should not pose any challenges and is likely to yield a satisfactory income.

A significant challenge associated with diversification exclusively through individual stock purchases is that it may reach a juncture where one's ability to effectively monitor them all diminishes. This phenomenon will occur at both the primary and secondary levels. You will be required to diligently maintain records of your stock portfolio, including monitoring their performance, dividend payments, and indicators such as the payout ratio. It is imperative that you also maintain up-to-date records of the company's financials. If it is not feasible for you to dedicate yourself to this task full-time, it will prove challenging to effectively monitor companies beyond a restricted number. You may also wish to consider exploring alternative investment opportunities in various companies.

In chapter 5, it will be demonstrated that a viable approach to circumvent this challenge resides in directing investments towards dividend-paying mutual funds or exchange traded funds. That method of investment is experiencing a growing trend in popularity, and it is justified by compelling reasons. Such investment options offer individuals the opportunity to gain automatic exposure to numerous companies, ranging from tens to even thousands, through a single investment.

Additionally, a considerable number of funds offer attractive dividend payments. Through the allocation of a portion of your finances into these particular funds, a substantial level of diversification can be attained, thereby insulating you from any adverse repercussions resulting from the potential insolvency of one or two entities. You have the option to incorporate certain funds into your overall investment portfolio, or alternatively, allocate all of your investments exclusively to funds.

In chapter 7, it will become evident that alternative methods exist for receiving dividend payments that do not necessitate the purchase of stock in typical large-scale, publicly traded corporations. In the forthcoming chapter, our discussion will encompass real estate investment trusts, master limited partnerships, and business development companies. Indeed, these entities are actively traded on prominent stock exchanges, providing investors with the invaluable advantage of gaining exposure to a highly diversified range of investments. This has the potential to bolster and fortify your portfolio.

Now, let us proceed to our discussion on sectors. When individuals contemplate diversification, they may envision the acquisition of a portfolio comprising twenty individual stocks, or alternatively, they may contemplate the acquisition of stocks in renowned companies such as Google, Facebook, Amazon, Apple, and so forth.

To rephrase this statement in a more formal tone: "To clarify, their intention entails the acquisition of a well-rounded assortment of stocks. However, they are primarily contemplating the procurement of stocks confined within a single industry." The aforementioned illustration pertains to the domain of advanced technology. However, in order to effectively establish a well-diversified portfolio, one must consider diversification beyond mere investments in various stocks. In addition, it is essential to consider diversifying one's investments across various sectors of the economy.

Frequently, there may be instances where a particular sector of the economy experiences a decline. Even during a severe economic downturn, certain industries experience more significant impacts than others. Take into account the repercussions of the 2008 financial crisis, which had a far-reaching impact on multiple sectors. While the impact was felt by all, it was the banking and financial industry that suffered disproportionately. If one were to hypothetically consider an investment strategy solely focused on the banking sector, it could be inferred that such a position would have yielded inferior outcomes compared to a diversified portfolio spanning multiple sectors. Other industries may have mitigated the extent of their decline to a lesser degree than the banking sector, and subsequently experienced a more expeditious recovery.

Invest Like The Sloth

Do you recall the admonition I gave you beforehand regarding the lethargic creature, the sloth? This creature possesses abysmal visual capabilities. However, it is permissible as it is not overly challenging to discern a suitable tree for suspension, a task that it executes adeptly owing to the elongated talons located at the terminus of each of its appendages. The sloth possesses deficient auditory capabilities, exhibits a metabolic rate considerably slower than that of vehicular movement in New York City, and ambulates at a maximum speed of merely ten meters every minute - under optimum circumstances. One cannot help but experience a modicum of empathy towards an animal burdened by such an overwhelming array of adversities. However, the sloth serves as a compelling metaphor for the concept of passive investing.

As an aspiring cautious investor, the ideal approach to passive investment strategy can be likened to that of the sloth: deliberate, consistent, and uncomplicated. This particular investment portfolio necessitates only a minute amount of time. Devoting occasional focus to redistributing the assets and expressing appreciation towards it.

Investing in index-linked portfolios (ETFs) can be viewed as a manifestation of one's faith in the broader economy. Based on my professional experience, I have identified three fundamental factors that contribute to the growth and advancement of the economy:

Technology will always evolve. Automobiles will witness advancements, medical science will triumph over a wider range of ailments, and engineers will innovate accelerated computing technologies.

Populations will multiply. Countries that experience a reduction in birthrates, like those in Western Europe, continue to pursue policies that promote immigration from regions characterized by higher birthrates. In nations characterized by a lack of significant population growth and inadequacies in immigration policies, such as Japan, economies predominantly experience a state of unchanging stability. An increase in population generally augments economic development.

Consumer tastes and preferences are subject to alteration. How many individuals among you don garments featuring lapels that extend beyond the proximal boundaries of your underarms? When was the most recent instance in which you unsealed a chilled container of Tab? Anyone? The transformation of consumer preferences has a positive impact on the economy, as it leads to increased employment opportunities, growth in sales, and gains in profitability.

Should these three conditions remain stable within the economic framework, or if at least some of them are upheld over a certain duration, there exists minimal justification for a decline in overall economic progress, notwithstanding occasional company failures. A corresponding claim can be formulated in regard to your passive ETF investments, characterized by sluggishness.

The Genesis of Dividends

In essence, a dividend can be likened to a form of rental income. Investors choose to acquire apartment buildings as investments due to the anticipated long-term financial gains they offer. You are likely to make a substantial initial investment to acquire the building; however, as time progresses, you will receive a monthly rental income that represents a modest proportion of its overall worth. Ingenious, isn't it? Moreover, the potential for future gains is not limited to the aforementioned benefits alone. In the long run, there exists the possibility that your property may appreciate, as the surrounding neighborhood becomes increasingly sought-after. Additionally, rental rates could ascend, inflationary pressures could take effect, and real estate bubbles might emerge — all outcomes that an astute investor would undoubtedly greet with great satisfaction.

Individuals engage in investments in companies for essentially the identical rationale that one would acquire an apartment building. You acquire ownership of a portion of a company (or multiple companies), and as a result, they remunerate you with a predetermined percentage of their earnings at regular intervals. In addition, it is pertinent to note that as companies undergo expansion and progress, the value of their stocks typically increases in tandem with their financial prosperity.

What are the reasons for the widespread appeal of real estate investment? The motivation behind acquiring property extends beyond mere status-oriented pursuits. In terms of investment, it represents a comprehensible and straightforward strategy.

Buy an apartment building.

Fill it with tenants.

Accumulate rental payments, and gradually augment the rental charges over a period.

The appreciation of your property is a result of the upward trajectory in real estate prices, thereby affording you supplementary profits should you opt to divest.

As previously stated, generating income from stocks bears resemblance to acquiring earnings from real estate.

Acquire equity in a corporation.

The company makes money.

The organization disseminates its generated funds among its proprietors or stakeholders in the form of dividends.

The firm's ongoing expansion and increased profitability result in a subsequent rise in its share price.

Please hold on! It should be noted that not all companies disburse dividends.

This is true. Nevertheless, the absence of dividend distribution by a company should not be misconstrued as an indicator of its lack of profitability or its insignificance as an investment opportunity. Technology companies that are publicly traded and experiencing rapid growth, like Amazon for instance, generally refrain from distributing dividends. This is due to the fact that it is more logical to reinvest their profits into the company to facilitate its growth and expansion. Apple stands out as a noteworthy exception to this. Since 2012, dividends have been distributed to investors by the company, as the newly appointed CEO, Tim Cook, held the belief that such payouts would serve as an enticement to draw in more investors. While Cook's predecessor and the founder of the company, Steve Jobs, held the belief that profits should be reinvested into ongoing product development.

The rationale behind the sustained operation of a company lies in its financial gains. In the absence of profitability, the possibility of the company going out of business becomes apparent. The index in which you choose to make an investment is subject to the same management principles. To illustrate this, let us consider the S&P 500, an index comprising the top 500 companies listed on the US stock exchanges. Given your familiarity with these companies, it is highly likely that you have engaged with their products or services as their esteemed customer. When a company listed on a US stock exchange achieves significant profitability, it is included in the S&P 500 index, displacing a comparatively less successful company. However, by investing in an index such as the S&P 500, you are exclusively allocating your investments towards these top-performing companies, eliminating the need for any research or deliberate decision-making on your part.

In the year 2020, Macy's, the renowned American department store chain, was excluded from the list owing to a significant decrease in its financial viability. Now envision a scene reminiscent of Hollywood, characterized by overused clichés, where all ETF shareholders who have invested in the S&P 500 collectively metaphorically discard the stock, symbolized by kicking it down the stairs, while vociferously proclaiming: 'Depart from my portfolio, Macy's! I have no tolerance for your justifications! Behold! We have already substituted you with a lucrative enterprise to generate profits for us!'

Sinister laughter resonates as the scene gradually transitions into darkness.

That is more or less what transpired.

Effective Financial Management: Mastering the Art of Expenditure and Savings

Until one gains a thorough grasp of cost management, achieving the designated savings goals shall remain unattainable. Failure to do so will result in your expenses depleting the entirety of your necessary savings.

In numerous respects, youth bestows a unique advantage as it typically entails minimal financial obligations. The financial obligations you have, such as bills, are covered by your parents or other responsible adults in your life. Hence, the income you generate is entirely at your disposal to spend as you deem appropriate. It shall not resemble that scenario once you reach adulthood. While your current expenditures may be minimal, it is prudent to make provisions for future financial obligations.

Charmaine intends to purchase a remote control car valued at $50 for her younger sibling, however, she has depleted all of her allotted daily funds instead of saving them. Charmaine had the desire to procure the remote control vehicle; however, her financial circumstances only allowed for the purchase of a $5 decal for a car.

In your opinion, do you believe that Charmaine's financial choices are prudent? Certainly not, as she fails to attain her true desires. On the contrary, she opts for an alternative that she finds even less agreeable.

What would be the optimal course of action for Charmaine to acquire possession of the remote control car? Charmaine should allocate a minimum amount of funds, even if it amounts to only $1 on a daily basis. After the course of 50 days, she will have accumulated a sum total of $50, thereby possessing ample financial resources to afford the desired toy.

Is it not more advantageous to acquire that which one genuinely desires, rather than compromising for what is currently within one's means? Notwithstanding this, numerous individuals, primarily adults, opt for substandard conditions in their lives.

It simply requires setting aside funds and discerning your long-term aspirations instead of succumbing to impulsive desires. Charmaine successfully acquired the toy on behalf of her younger sibling. Wouldn't this alternative approach be more suitable for her to manage her finances?

Nelson, for instance, possesses a total of $20 in his possession. He desires a sticker book; however, it is imperative for him to acquire a math textbook. The cost of both books is $20 each. Nelson's mother is prepared to gift him a sum of $20 in the event that he attains an "A" grade on his forthcoming arithmetic examination. Nelson currently possesses a distinct and definitive option. He has the option to immediately utilize his $20 to purchase a sticker book, or he can opt to invest it in the acquisition of an arithmetic textbook that would enable him to achieve an "A" grade and subsequently receive an additional sum of $20 from his mother. What course of action would one pursue if they were in Nelson's position? Should he opt for the second alternative, it would undoubtedly entail a certain degree of risk and necessitate some effort. Despite Nelson's potential purchase of the math book, his test performance may still result in failure. However, the likelihood of him achieving an "A" significantly decreases if he opts not to acquire the book.

Nelson must acquire the mathematics textbook and dedicate considerable effort to studying using his newly obtained resource in order to achieve an "A" grade. In the end, Nelson made the decision to procure the mathematics textbook. He achieved a grade of "A" and as a reward, his mother gifted him with $20 to purchase the sticker book.

Another factor to be taken into account is whether Nelson should have opted for buying the math textbook, even if it entailed sacrificing the sticker book. You possess exclusive knowledge regarding the resolution of that particular inquiry. An additional approach to acquire insights on expenditure patterns would involve closely observing the financial behaviors of adults in your vicinity. Display courtesy while expressing curiosity about their expenditure choices.

May I suggest that you offer help by providing cost-effective alternatives that could assist them in economizing. Rather than allocating funds towards extravagant dining experiences, it may be suggested that your parents consider investing in a modest yet exceptional lunch.

Thus, could you kindly disclose the key to cultivating exemplary financial practices? Postponing our immediate gratification to strategize for our future requirements and contentment. This phenomenon is occasionally denoted as postponing immediate satisfaction.

Utilizing The Potential Within Negativity "

Buffett is widely recognized for his consistently positive outlook on the United States, its potential to overcome adversity and setbacks. During the peak of panic and fear in the autumn of 2008, when the markets were engulfed in turmoil, Buffett emerged as a prominent national advocate. He authored an opinion editorial, titled "Buy American," that was published in the prestigious publication known as the New York Times. I am, as of October 2008. In the article, he expressed that amidst the tumultuous circumstances, undervalued American companies were available at remarkably affordable prices, prompting him to consider making additional purchases for his portfolio, despite his portfolio already comprising several high-performing American companies.

The inquiry arises as to why Buffett would openly proclaim his sentiment of "Buy American" amidst such a challenging period. He undertook this action with the conviction that "apprehensions pertaining to the sustained success of numerous reputable companies within the country are unfounded." Buffett explicitly refrained from making a "market forecast" or anticipating an imminent reversal of fortunes in the stock market.

He expressed uncertainty regarding the timing of the market's resurgence, but emphasized his belief that it would inevitably happen. And when it occurred, you desired to be counted as one of the courageous investors who made purchases during the most dismal periods. Buffett unquestionably possesses an innate optimism, yet he astutely acknowledges and capitalizes on the notion that periods characterized by pessimism hold the potential to yield lucrative opportunities for long-term investors. It is probable that this will be the outcome for investors who heeded Buffett's guidance and purchased stocks during a period in autumn 2008 when the global situation appeared to be deteriorating. In alignment with his earlier statements, expressed in a New York Times article, he reiterated that unfavorable developments hold significant value for investors. It affords one the opportunity to acquire a portion of America's forthcoming prospects at a discounted rate." He further expressed, "In the realm of investments, having a pessimistic outlook is advantageous, while succumbing to euphoria proves detrimental." In his shareholder letter of 2009, Buffett reiterated his stance, stating, "An atmosphere of apprehension is the greatest ally for investors.

Individuals who engage in investment solely based on the optimism expressed by commentators often incur significant costs for obtaining reassurance that lacks substantial value. Ultimately, the crucial factor in investing lies in the valuation of a business, achieved through acquiring a fractional ownership in the company's stock and assessing the subsequent earnings of said business over the course of a decade or two. Nevertheless, Buffett exerts caution in order to prevent his intrinsic optimism from impairing his discernment. He displays a consistent composure in response to his investments and the volatilities of the market. His esteemed mentor, Benjamin Graham, expounded upon a fictional persona known as "Mr. Market," who presented himself as a reliable interlocutor accessible on a daily basis. Mr. Market featured as a willing counterparty, proffering a range of prices to either purchase existing shares from you or facilitate the acquisition of novel ones. In the event that you declined his proposal on a certain day, there would be no inconvenience as he would reappear on the subsequent day with an alternative offer. Buffett has expressed a fondness for this analogy and has consistently imparted this lesson to investors, emphasizing their authority over Mr. Market rather than the other way around.

It is essential not to become excessively agitated by his indecisive actions in either direction. This mindset is furthermore instrumental in enabling Buffett to steer clear of episodes characterized by excessive excitement and irrationality, such as the technology boom witnessed in the 1990s. Buffett did not share the boundless optimism that investors had regarding technology during that period. In his 1979 article for Forbes, he articulated that the certainty of the future is always obscured. A substantial cost is incurred in the realm of stock market investments when seeking a unanimous and optimistic viewpoint. "Indeterminate outcomes provide advantageous opportunities for individuals seeking to acquire assets with long-term growth potential." Graham's investment ideology was rooted in a negative outlook, a perspective that Buffett gradually distanced himself from over time. Termed as the "cigar butt" investment strategy, the concept revolved around identifying stocks at their absolute lowest valuation (such as companies trading below the fair market value of their assets), and acquiring shares with the expectation of extracting some residual value, akin to salvaging the last remaining puffs from a discarded cigar one fortuitously stumbles upon (which may appear unappealing upon contemplation).

This particular ideological framework failed to take into account the caliber of the organization's leadership, the prospects of the enterprise, or the robustness of its brand or competitive edge. The primary focus was strictly on assessing the "margin of safety." Graham's approach can be characterized as cautious, as it did not involve seeking out long-term investment prospects that would allow for both personal and generational benefits, such as benefiting from their competitive advantages and observing their growth potential. No, on the contrary, you were simply strolling with a downward gaze, seeking momentary indulgences here and there, devoid of any long-term vision, devoid of optimism for the prospects of the business in the coming days. To a certain extent, Buffett's shift in perspective can be attributed to the guidance of his business associate, Charlie Munger. This has led him to move beyond his pessimistic outlook and instead focus on identifying robust enterprises with promising prospects. However, he refrained from succumbing to an overly optimistic perspective. He consistently maintains a pragmatic approach in evaluating companies, avoiding unrealistic expectations and not seeking out undervalued opportunities with limited potential.

Principle of Supply and Demand

It is expected that you possess knowledge of the fact that in the field of economics, a surplus of a product typically leads to a decline in its associated price. The lack of consumer demand for the product renders any company, or in this specific instance, a stock, unappealing.

In instances of inadequate supply such as with a stock, the level of demand considerably rises. As the number of stakeholders grows, the price will inevitable surge.

In the event that the quantity of supply matches the quantity of demand, a state of equilibrium is achieved, resulting in a lack of observable changes.

In the context of the stock market, an excessive number of traders offloading a particular stock leads to a subsequent decrease in its price. As the number of stock purchasers increases, the price will perpetually ascend. In the event that there is a parity between the number of shares and interest, it is customary for the price to exhibit horizontal movement, as equilibrium is maintained.

In the process of acquiring knowledge about the stock market, you will frequently encounter the term volume. Volume refers to the quantity of shares that are traded within a given day. In a single trading day, a substantial volume of shares can be exchanged on the stock market as investors endeavor to capitalize on price fluctuations in order to generate profits.

The functioning of the stock market is contingent upon the level of interest or the magnitude of participation exhibited by traders. In the event that a stock exhibits negligible or no trading volume, it can be inferred that it is not subject to active trading, resulting in limited price fluctuations. Traders such as market makers participate in the market with the intention of executing stock transactions on behalf of companies characterized by low trading volumes. They do not impede the upward or downward movement of a stock. Alternatively, market makers primarily endeavor to generate interest in the company's stock.

What the majority of individuals commonly engage in

Regarding the stock market and traders, the majority of individuals are seeking trades with high trading volume and prices that are subject to fluctuations. They enter, generate revenue, and depart in search of the next lucrative opportunity.

Final Thoughts

The company initiates the issuance of shares in order to secure funds through investment. The shares are subsequently exchanged, serving as a means to accrue dividends and capitalize on the fluctuations within the market. Additionally, the market offers the opportunity to engage in investment activities on multiple global exchanges, contingent upon your broker's provision of access. The majority of individuals engage in trading within the stock market of their respective countries or in prominent regional stock exchanges such as the Japan Stock Exchange, London Stock Exchange, and NYSE.

Candlestick

An additional instrument to incorporate into your repertoire would be the candlestick, renowned for its utility as a price chart employed for the purpose of technical analysis. It presents a comprehensive depiction of the security's high, low, open, and closing prices during a specified timeframe. They have a tendency to indicate to investors whether the closing price of a market was lower or higher than its opening price, a critical factor in comprehending the true performance of the stock market. Consequently, it proves to be highly advantageous for traders who are specifically seeking out chart patterns that may potentially arise.

The term "candlestick" is derived from the market's visual representation, which closely resembles the shape of a traditional candlestick. The appellation originated from Japanese rice merchants and other traders who exhibited advanced proficiency in documenting financial management prior to its popularization in America.

The uppermost point of the candlestick symbolizes the peak price attained during the day, while the lowermost point of the candlestick signifies the nadir price reached within the same day. The more substantial central element located at the upper section denotes the commencement and conclusion values, as does the weightier component observed at the lower part. If the stock concludes at a lower price, the candlestick's body assumes a black or red hue, while a higher closing price manifests as a white or green body for the candlestick.

The candlestick's silhouette symbolizes the fluctuations experienced throughout the day, specifically when juxtaposed with the openings and closings of the stock market.

In essence, the candlestick symbolizes the investor's influence on security prices and is frequently employed for technical analysis, given its direct correlation with the company's financial standing in the stock market. This tool serves as a convenient resource for individuals engaged in penny stock investing, and it is advisable to acquire comprehensive knowledge about it prior to venturing into the realm of investment. Candlesticks serve as a valuable tool in a variety of trading methodologies, encompassing various types of financial instruments including equities and foreign currencies.

When the candlestick exhibits a white or green color, it typically indicates a substantial increase in buying pressure on a specific stock. This often serves as an indication that a specific stock is displaying a bullish trend. However, it is crucial to analyze the candlestick pattern within the broader market framework, as it can offer valuable insights into the factors that may influence your decision to invest or refrain from investing. When one observes a significant number of red or green candlesticks, it serves as an indication of prevalent selling pressure and signifies the market being in a state of bearish sentiment. What is the significance of a market being in a "bearish" or "bullish" condition?

A bull market refers to a condition where a stock's value demonstrates a discernible upward trend and trades in a more consistent manner. This situation typically serves as an advantageous opportunity for traders, particularly those who are prioritizing a long-term strategy.

A bearish market is indicative of a decline in prices, prompting a significant number of individuals to express a desire to divest their stock holdings. Surprisingly, individuals can also derive advantages from this phenomenon by engaging in short selling. However, engaging in this mode of profit generation entails considerably higher risk and necessitates a substantial level of expertise to successfully execute such endeavors.

Now returning to the topic of the candlestick: Traders have the opportunity to leverage candlestick charts as a highly effective means of analyzing all trading cycles that may occur at any given moment within a day. One can also employ it to examine a short span of trading, ranging from a single minute to a maximum of one hour. It is entirely within your purview to employ these resources according to your judgment and prudence. In summary, there is a wealth of knowledge to be gained in the realm of candle charts, and their value is expected to endure well into the future.

Overview Of Virtual Reality Technology

Virtual refers to a state of non-physicality, whereby individuals engage in the virtual realm through computers to experience and interact with non-existing elements of life. This entails merely traversing a realm that does not align with reality. If you were to view depictions of paintings from the war era and allow yourself to immerse in their essence, it is plausible that you might conjure up the auditory sensations of gunfire reverberating through the air, among other aspects. Similarly, when one listens to classical or instrumental music with closed eyes and begins to envision scenarios, they are experiencing a form of virtual reality. Have you considered envisioning the occurrences depicted in a film or literary work? It appears to be a manifestation of virtual reality. But it isn't. Engaging in the act of reading, watching films, or envisioning the events depicted in a painting merely retains their presence within the realm of one's thoughts or mind, devoid of tangible sensations or active participation in the book's narrative.

Virtual reality is an immersive simulated environment generated by computer technology, allowing users to engage and navigate through a three-dimensional realm in a manner that induces both physical and psychological sensations. In the realm of virtual environments, it is imperative to engender a steadfast belief in an alternate reality, diligently maintaining this conviction to ensure the preservation of the simulated world's verisimilitude. Additionally, it is imperative to maintain a high degree of interactivity, as the virtual reality environment seamlessly adapts to your movements and actions. One can engage in reading a book and be immersed in the depiction of the sea without attaining a genuine sense of being transported, thereby lacking sufficient interactivity. In order for a virtual world to provide an enriching experience, it must possess considerable expanse and an abundance of intricate elements, enabling extensive exploration opportunities. It is imperative that the content is captivating. It is imperative to ensure a high level of interactivity and believability, fostering deep engagement of both the physical and cognitive faculties. The works of artists who depict war provide us with a visual interpretation of the nature of conflict, yet they are unable to fully capture the entirety of the sensory experience, including the auditory, visual, gustatory, and olfactory dimensions, as well as the profound impact of being actively engaged in warfare. You have the opportunity to engage in a virtual reality game that offers an immersive, lifelike, and interactive experience lasting approximately two hours.

Based on the aforementioned points, it is evident that engaging with paintings, immersing oneself in a beloved literary work, or partaking in a cinematic experience are fundamentally distinct from the realm of virtual reality. Each of them affords a limited glimpse into an alternative reality; however, none of them are capable of being explored or interacted with. Imagine that you are engrossed in a film, fixated on a grand depiction of a conflict unfolding prominently before you, and subsequently divert your gaze to attend to a task. Under such circumstances, you will come to realize that you are, indeed, still situated on the planet Earth. The illusion will dissipate if you happen upon something visually captivating on the screen, as you will be incapable of physically interacting with it or returning to its location. That illusion will gradually dissipate. Consequently, engaging in movie viewing is considered a rather passive endeavor, as it limits active involvement in the events unfolding on screen.

Virtual reality is different. It imbues the perception of residing within our reality; the unparalleled interactivity enables a reciprocal effect, whereby one's actions upon sight and touch engender corresponding reactions. By altering one's trajectory, the scenery and auditory perception adapt synchronously to align with the new vantage point.

The Utilization Of Virtual Reality

There is a prevalent belief among many individuals that virtual reality holds no utility beyond its application in gaming. This assertion lacks complete accuracy as virtual reality finds additional applications beyond the one mentioned. Virtual reality is not purely a realm of fantasy and amusement, bereft of any educational value. There is a plethora of pertinent knowledge to be gained from it, making it a valuable resource for professionals seeking information and conducting comprehensive research. For the past two decades, professionals such as dentists, engineers, archaeologists, doctors, paramilitary personnel, and various other experts have been employing virtual reality technology as a means to effectively address complex challenges. In the course of its evolution, virtual reality technology has found applications in scientific presentations and training programs. Furthermore, it is worth noting that doctors frequently employ it in the context of anatomy and surgical training. Virtual reality is an indispensable tool for architects in the process of designing a model of a building.

Are you aware that virtual reality has the potential to significantly transform our lives in the near future?

In the near future, a transformation awaits each person's life with regards to virtual reality, given its multifaceted advantages and possibilities. Virtual reality technologies are continuously progressing, and it is anticipated that global dissemination of information and knowledge that could impact our lives will ensue. If individuals were to universally adopt virtual reality, it would enable widespread accessibility to education regardless of geographical location, facilitating the dissemination of acquired knowledge among diverse global communities. The implementation of the virtual reality training program will effectively eliminate classroom distractions, ensuring that students remain focused on their learning without any external interruptions.

Physicians, including surgeons, will enhance their skill sets and intellectual capabilities, thereby striving for mastery in their profession. Virtual surgery training primarily entails the utilization of a virtual reality interface, which offers interactive models afflicted with diverse ailments requiring surgical intervention. This platform enables surgeons to enhance their surgical skills and effectively carry out the corresponding procedures.

Virtual reality will additionally provide individuals with the opportunity to partake in a simulated journey, devoid of any physical displacement from their abodes. The emergence of the Metaverse becomes relevant in this particular scenario. One can engage in travel, social activities, shopping, and even vacate their residences. Virtual reality will additionally provide individuals with a heightened sense of convenience as they engage in remote work from the comfort of their own residences. With the development of virtual reality applications, individuals are able to perform tasks remotely, maintaining uninterrupted connectivity to the digital printer, thereby facilitating an immersive and uninterrupted work experience.

Approach Thirteen: Procuring Goods for the Geriatric Population

The continuously expanding demographic of individuals aged 65 and above mandates a corresponding elevation in the provisions offered to the elderly. A food procurement service is a highly favored option for aiding the elderly. Elderly individuals who are unable to operate a vehicle or who are experiencing medical difficulties may find themselves confined to their homes. When it comes to everyday tasks such as grocery shopping, they necessitate aid.

Younger individuals might perceive shopping as an enjoyable pursuit, whereas older individuals are more inclined to perceive it as onerous, particularly when they are required to visit multiple establishments for essential items such as groceries and medications. Some individuals employ personal shoppers to attend to their shopping needs. If you are prepared to establish a business, your inherent passion for shopping can serve as a means to generate income. The sole requirement for employment in this particular sector is the capacity to negotiate effectively and possess a fundamental sense of practicality.

A business plan focused on personal shopping services will suffice. If you possess prior experience in grocery shopping for personal use, you will encounter no difficulties in fulfilling the duties of an individual assisting older adults with their shopping needs. To successfully initiate a personal shopping enterprise, it is imperative that you

• Pick a specialty. One advantage of working in this industry is the abundance of opportunities available, although it may pose a challenge to fully engage in all of them. It is advisable to focus on a limited number of specialized markets. Purchasing groceries is unequivocally the most prevalent undertaking. Senior citizens could potentially experience advantages from the assistance of a dedicated individual who attends to their shopping needs at the supermarket.

• Procure the essential commodities required for your shopping expedition. In this company, only a reliable mode of transportation such as a bicycle will be necessary. Bicycles or electric bikes are highly advantageous as they offer ample storage capacity for transporting cargo. Furthermore, it would be advantageous for your professional phone to be equipped with a camera as there may be occasions when you require concrete evidence to confirm purchases. Having a camera phone at your disposal would facilitate this process. If you currently lack such a device, it would be advisable to request permission from your parents to procure an affordable and high-performing one, solely designated for the purposes of executing your business functions.

• Promote your brand. In the initial stages, there is a need for diligent efforts in order to obtain clientele and establish rapport, but subsequently, as your customer network expands through word-of-mouth referrals, the level of exertion required diminishes. To effectively attract customers, it is advisable to prioritize targeting locations that are commonly visited by senior individuals. You may also consider disseminating your brochures at senior centers in strategic positions that capture individuals' attention, enticing them to pick them up as they depart from the premises. You can explore a wide range of alternatives, encompassing retirement facilities, medical centers, wellness establishments, insurance agencies, and an array of additional possibilities.

• Disclose your current activities transparently. Truthfulness and transparency are crucial attributes that will greatly contribute to your advancement in your professional endeavors. Instill a sense of trust in your customers by presenting yourself as someone genuinely invested in their concerns and capable of offering viable solutions, rather than solely driven by monetary gain. It is imperative to demonstrate patience and provide a considerable level of support and understanding while interacting with older adults.

TIP

As an individual engaged in personal shopping, you possess the ability to set your hourly rate at an upper limit of $20 per hour for the services rendered.

Procedure Fourteen: Furniture Cleaning

The act of sanitizing objects like mattresses, sofas, and chairs could also be characterized as the process of purifying furniture. Homeowners often exhibit hesitation in undertaking this task, as it necessitates a substantial investment of time and exertion.

Efforts should be made to persuade homeowners who have canine companions to avail themselves of your service. It will enable you to enhance your financial gains. There is an increased likelihood that furniture cleaning will be prioritized by individuals who own pets.

● Develop a homemade cleansing solution utilizing dish soap. To ensure appropriate utilization, incorporate water into a spray bottle, and thereafter, introduce two drops of liquid dish soap. The application of vinegar and baking soda for the purpose of neutralizing odors will consistently prove effective. Blend it vigorously.

• In order to remove surface dirt and dust, it is advisable to perform regular dusting of the furniture. It is necessary to remove any residual surface dirt.

Commence by utilizing the mildest detergent and subsequently progress to stronger alternatives, if necessary.

• Cleanse the object by using a cloth that has been moistened and subsequently squeezed to remove excess moisture. Given your preference to avoid wetting your hands, it would be more desirable for you to use a moist towel instead of a wet one.

In order to achieve a uniform and smooth surface, it is advised not to excessively saturate the wood and to regularly clean the dust cloth.

Kindly exercise patience momentarily, and subsequently proceed to thoroughly dry the object utilizing a fresh cloth.

When undertaking the task of cleaning conventional furniture –

• Employ thorough cleaning techniques to eradicate dust and eliminate deceased skin cells from upholstered furniture, including meticulously scrubbing all the intricate spaces and gaps within the cushions. Thoroughly vacuum the cushions and remove all of the cushion covers prior to utilizing a washcloth for scrubbing. Utilize a sponge to absorb blemishes. While administering the concoction, thoroughly knead it into the surface using a sponge. Concurrently, ensure to promptly absorb any moisture on your furniture by employing a towel.

• Utilize a vacuum cleaner to attend to the maintenance of leather furniture. Please employ the soft brush attachment when cleaning the furniture with a vacuum to ensure its preservation. Regularly employing vacuuming techniques aids in the maintenance of furniture by ensuring the cleanliness of both the surfaces and upholstery. To ensure a thorough cleaning of the furniture, it is recommended to remove the padding, allowing access to all corners.

- When it comes to acrylic and lucite furniture, employ a pristine cloth. Accumulation of dirt and grime can cause substantial harm to acrylic and lucite. The utilization of a new fabric could potentially serve as a preventive measure against the formation of scratches.

Index Fund Categories

A notable aspect of index funds lies in their varied classifications, which do not conform to any singular category. There exist various categories of these funds that can cater to individuals' preferences. The inaugural index fund was established in 1976, and it has witnessed progressive diversification and increased intricacy in subsequent years. These diverse categories of index funds provide investors with a means to access supplementary markets, sectors, and investment approaches.

Broad Market:

This particular index aims to encompass a significant portion of the market for investment purposes. These investments encompass equities, fixed-income securities, and any other form of financial instrument. Broad market indexes exhibit significantly low expense ratios, and due to the minimal frequency of security turnover, they offer substantial tax efficiency. This fund offers a highly varied assortment of securities. Should you opt to make an investment in the broader market, exercise caution with regards to maintaining holdings in other indexes. There might be certain duplications in your selected securities.

International:

International index funds have the potential to offer substantial external exposure to your investment portfolio. Numerous broad market indexes predominantly emphasize companies based in the United States. By leveraging the international index, investors can avail themselves of the advantageous prospects offered by companies across

Europe, Africa, Asia, Australia, and Oceania. Antarctica is the sole location that is not available for purchase. These categories of funds do not necessarily exhibit a direct affiliation with specific geographical regions such as the Middle East or Central America.

Term-based Bonds:

These investment opportunities cater to individuals with a preference for long-term investments. The inclusion of a well-balanced assortment of short, intermediate, and long-term bonds can yield a consistent and prolonged income stream.

Municipal Bonds:

These bonds do not incur federal taxes and frequently enjoy exemptions from state and local taxes as well. The latter condition holds solely in cases where the bond is issued within the domicile of the respective investor. If you happen to reside in a jurisdiction characterized by elevated state and local taxes, it would be advisable to focus exclusively on seeking bonds of such nature within your designated locality. This will help insulate you from the substantial deduction of taxes.

Earnings-based:

This section encompasses two distinct categories of indexes: growth indexes and value indexes. Composite indices comprise businesses with a projected ability to enhance their earnings at a greater pace compared to the broader market. Value indexes consist of stocks that exhibit a low price in relation to the company's earnings. Growth stocks exhibit significantly higher levels of volatility in comparison to value stocks, leading to rapid ascents during market upswings and swift declines during market downturns. Due to the fact that value stocks possess lower prices, their decline is relatively insignificant during market downturns. Additionally, they exhibit a delay in keeping pace with the broader market's upward movement.

Sectors:

It is within your discretion to opt for investment opportunities in particular verticals of the market, such as the realm of real estate. The sectors may encompass a wide range of industries, such as technology, or may be more narrowly focused, for example, on cloud computing. Numerous investors seek to gain exposure to a specific industry, yet lack certainty in selecting the most suitable one. Thus, individuals have the opportunity to invest in a sector-specific fund, enabling the market to determine the most favorable company to invest in.

Based on the information presented, it is evident that Index funds offer an extensive range of choices for your investment portfolio. Although there are certain limitations on specific criteria when you actively engage, you still have a wide array of options at your disposal prior to initiating your participation. Furthermore, it is worth noting that simultaneous possession of multiple indexes is permissible, as long as caution is exercised to prevent any duplication of individual securities within them.

Dividend-Focused:

A dividend is a recurring monetary payment, typically disbursed periodically, and commonly on a quarterly interval. Herein lie two distinct categories: growth and yield. Dividend growth indexes encompass companies that maintain a consistent track record of increasing their dividends and demonstrate the potential to continue doing so in forthcoming iterations. Dividend yield indexes consist of stocks that possess a substantial yield in terms of dividends. These index funds are ideal for investors who are seeking a reliable source of income from their investments.

Your Exchange Could Potentially Be Associated With A Designated Method Of Payment.

Once you have made a decision regarding the exchange, please proceed to collect your personal documents. Additional data that may be transmitted encompasses visual representations of your driver's license or Social Security identification, as well as details regarding your employment and income level. The information needed may vary depending on your place of residency and the prevailing legislation in your locality. Establishing a brokerage account involves a similar process.

Once your identification has been verified by the exchange, you will be prompted to establish a connection with a payment method. If you wish to utilize a debit or credit card for the purpose of depositing funds, it is permissible to do so at the majority of exchanges. Whilst it remains a possibility to acquire cryptocurrency through the use of a credit card, it is advisable to exercise caution in light of the unpredictable fluctuations witnessed within the cryptocurrency market, which have the potential to augment the overall expenses incurred during the acquisition of a coin.

Whilst it remains within the boundaries of legality to utilize Bitcoin in the United States, financial institutions may exercise meticulous examination or potentially impede the act of depositing funds to websites or exchanges associated with cryptocurrencies. It is advisable to confirm with your bank regarding the acceptance of deposits at the preferred currency exchange, as a measure of prudence.

Deposits can be facilitated through a bank account, debit card, or credit card. For initiation, Coinbase imposes a fee of 1.49 percent for bank account transfers and a charge of 3.99 percent for debit and credit card transactions. To arrive at an educated choice regarding the utilization of an exchange platform or a particular payment method, it is imperative to carefully assess the associated costs.

Exchanges also impose transaction fees. The fee structure will vary based on the magnitude of the transaction, with the possibility of it being a fixed amount or a percentage of the transaction value. Furthermore, aside from the incurred transactional expenses, there exists an accompanying processing fee correlated with the utilization of a credit card.

6.1.3 Facilitate a Transaction

Bitcoin (as well as other cryptocurrencies) can be readily acquired by choosing a suitable exchange platform and setting up an account. Over the past few years, there has been a gradual increase in the prevalence of cryptocurrency exchanges. They have experienced significant growth in both liquidity and the range of features they offer. In conjunction with the evolving public perception of cryptocurrencies, cryptocurrency exchanges are implementing operational adaptations. The financial services industry is beginning to acknowledge a business that was previously perceived as fraudulent or questionable, but is now regarded as reputable.

In alternative phrasing, it can be expressed as follows: "In other words, cryptocurrency trading platforms have now become comparable in terms of their level of functionality to traditional stock brokerages." Currently, there exists a multitude of order types and investment strategies that can be employed for cryptocurrency investment purposes. The majority of cryptocurrency exchanges offer the functionality to execute market and limit orders, as well as stop-loss orders, across a wide range of available options. Kraken possesses the highest variety of order types among the aforementioned exchanges. You have the option to utilize Kraken to execute market orders, limit orders, stop losses, and stop limits.

In addition to various order types, exchanges also provide customers with the opportunity to systematically invest in the assets of their preference through the utilization of recurring investments. An exemplary illustration would be the capacity to arrange regular purchases within Coinbase.

6.1.4 Preservation of Data in a Protected Setting

Wallets designed for Bitcoin and other cryptocurrencies offer a secure sanctuary for the preservation of digital assets. When the cryptocurrency is placed within a private wallet, exclusive ownership of the private key necessary to unlock one's assets is retained solely by the individual. In the event that your exchange encounters a security breach, apprehensions regarding financial losses need not arise as you can choose to maintain your funds in alternative locations.

Although many exchanges offer wallets to their customers, their primary emphasis is not directed towards ensuring security. It is generally advised against utilizing an exchange wallet for the purpose of long-term bitcoin holdings.

One can obtain wallets that offer an extensive array of choices. Certain individuals solely possess Bitcoin, while others offer the capacity to securely hold a diverse range of alternative digital currencies. It is feasible to engage in currency conversion within specific digital wallets.

There is a wide array of options at your disposal when it comes to selecting a Bitcoin wallet. To utilize a cryptocurrency wallet proficiently, it is imperative to acquire a comprehensive understanding of the distinction between a "hot wallet" (an online wallet) and a "cold wallet" (paper or hardware wallets).

Hot wallet

The phrase "hot wallet" pertains to digital wallets that are accessible online. The term "hot wallet" refers to a digital wallet that can be accessed via the internet, encompassing devices like computers, smartphones, and tablets. These wallets generate the private keys for your funds on these internet-enabled devices, thereby engendering a susceptibility. Although it is convenient to have accessibility and conduct transactions with your assets using a hot wallet, the exposure of your private key on a device connected to the internet heightens the risk of it being compromised in an attack.

Individuals who fail to employ sufficient security measures when utilizing these hot wallets are subject to the potential loss of their monetary assets. This is a not an infrequent occurrence, and there are multiple methods by which it might transpire. Engaging in public discussions on platforms such as Reddit and openly boasting about one's bitcoin holdings, particularly when storing them in a readily accessible online wallet, is not advisable. Nevertheless, if proper precautions are taken, the security of these wallets can be ensured. It is imperative to incorporate a range of prudent security measures, such as implementing two-factor authentication, utilizing robust passwords, and exercising vigilance in online activities.

These wallets are recommended for individuals possessing a limited number of cryptocurrencies or engaged in active trading on an exchange. A hot wallet can be likened to a conventional banking account. In accordance with traditional financial wisdom, it is advised to maintain only a nominal sum of money within a checking account, while allocating the remaining funds to a savings account or alternative investment account. In regard to heated wallets, the same assertion can be made. Hot wallets encompass various forms such as mobile wallets, desktop wallets, online wallets, and exchange account custody wallets.

As aforementioned, exchange wallets are custodial accounts provided by the exchange entity. The user of this particular wallet type does not possess ownership of the private key associated with the cryptocurrency held within. In the event of a security breach or unauthorized access to your account, there is a risk of losing your funds. Within the bitcoin forums and groups, it is frequently observed that the phrase "not your key, not your coin" is commonly employed.

Cold wallets

Regarding cold wallets, an alternative manner to articulate their nature would be to convey that they lack connectivity to the internet, thereby diminishing their susceptibility to unauthorized intrusion by hackers. Additionally, offline wallets and hardware wallets can be employed to denote these types of wallets. Provided the wallet remains disconnected from the internet, it is possible to safely store a user's private key within it without subjecting it to any risk.

When considering offline bitcoin storage, a paper wallet can be regarded as the most secure choice. Certain online platforms offer the capability to generate a paper-based wallet, in which you can subsequently safeguard your digital currency. Upon a piece of paper, it generates both public and private keys. Lacking possession of the private key will result in an inability to retrieve the bitcoin stored at the designated addresses. A considerable number of individuals opt to laminate these paper wallets and securely store them either in their bank's safe deposit box or within a home safe. The wallets mentioned above are highly recommended for individuals seeking long-term investment solutions. This is primarily due to the fact that bitcoin stored in these wallets cannot be readily sold or exchanged.

Regarding cold wallets, hardware wallets are the most commonly utilized. It is customary for hardware wallets to constitute USB drives that securely store a user's private keys offline. In contrast to hot wallets, which are susceptible to computer viruses, cold wallets remain immune to viral threats. By utilizing hardware wallets, your private keys remain isolated, safeguarded from any potential exposure to your network-connected computer or potentially vulnerable applications. Furthermore, these devices frequently embrace open source principles, facilitating the community's ability to authenticate their safety through rigorous code audits rather than solely depending on assurances from a specific company.

When considering the storage of cryptocurrency, cold wallets are the optimal choice. Nevertheless, configuring them necessitates further expertise.

It is recommended to establish an exchange account, utilize a hot wallet, and incorporate a cold hardware wallet into your wallet configuration to securely store moderate to substantial amounts of cryptocurrency intended for trading or selling purposes.

How To Engage In Bond Investment

This section is designed to provide instruction on four distinct methods for engaging in bond investments. Additionally, this discussion will elucidate the crucial variables and approaches that necessitate careful consideration when acquiring assets of this nature.

Four Approaches to Obtaining Bonds

Acquire individual bonds – These securities are frequently purchased and traded in over-the-counter financial markets. Nevertheless, certain bonds, particularly those issued by corporations, are accessible within the confines of the New York Stock Exchange. This asset is available for purchase from financial institutions and entities engaged in bond trading. You may also consider engaging the services of a broker agent, who can facilitate the buying or selling of individual bonds on your behalf.

Acquire shares from a bond fund entity – Such an entity consolidates the capital contributed by diverse investors and utilizes the funds to procure bonds. These companies offer expert assessment and administration of bond portfolios. If one lacks the time or inclination to personally oversee investment activities, this option is most suitable.

Allocate resources to Money Market Funds - These funds comprise aggregated capital intended for investment in short-term and highly dynamic assets. Below, I have provided a list of various asset types that exemplify the mentioned categories: government-issued securities (such as U.S. Treasuries), fixed-income instruments offered by municipalities, debt instruments issued by corporations known as commercial papers, and certificates of deposits (CODs) issued by commercial banks. Typically, the bonds in question yield profits within a span of 3 months.

Allocate funds to Bond Unit Investment Trusts – These entities offer pre-determined investment portfolios consisting of meticulously selected and expertly managed municipal, corporate, government, and mortgage-backed bonds. One of the key advantages presented by a unit investment trust resides in the certainty it provides, as it affords you a precise and predetermined understanding of the earnings you can expect to receive. This is feasible due to the consistent composition of the bond portfolio. Modifications are maintained at a minimum level.

The Factors That Require Deliberation

Diversification facilitates the dispersion and mitigation of risks inherent in your bond investment portfolio. Irrespective of your financial goals and investment approaches, it is imperative to ensure that your portfolio is adequately diversified. One can achieve diversification in bond investments by:

Utilizing a laddering strategy, you will allocate your capital towards both short-term and long-term bonds. Short-term bonds mitigate risks, whereas long-term bonds enable the investor to achieve substantial gains. After the expiration of the short-term bonds, it is advisable to "sustain the ladder" by allocating your funds into long-term bonds.

Diversifying your bond investments - It is advisable to purchase bonds from various industry sectors. This will aid in safeguarding and preserving the integrity of your investment portfolio. For example, in the event of a decline in price occurring within a specific sector, the remaining bonds within your portfolio will counterbalance and mitigate the adverse consequences.

- It is imperative to contemplate the approach for managing your bond investments, encompassing both active and passive management strategies. Certain individuals prefer to engage in frequent modifications to their investment portfolios, an approach commonly referred to as active portfolio management. Their acquisitions, disposals, and arrangement of portfolio holdings undergo regular modification.

Nevertheless, there are individuals who seek to mitigate the extent of alterations to their investments. These investors employ a method known as "buy and hold." Within this strategy, the investor exercises discernment in selecting bonds that will be acquired and retained until they generate profits.

About Discounting

The value of the cash you receive tomorrow will not be equivalent to the value of what you possess presently. This is the methodology employed by the value investor to ascertain the suitability of making a purchase today. The focus lies on the prospective projections of cash flow and earnings that a stock is poised to generate. The genuine value investor is primarily focused on computing the stock price as the aggregate of all future cash flows generated on a per-share basis. Due to the time value of money, the present value of anticipated cash flows exceeds the current stock value.

Consider the scenario where you possess an investment that yields a monetary return of one dollar in the present, as well as in the subsequent years. One must apply a discount rate that is appropriate in order to account for the time value of each dollar. The aforementioned formula essentially transforms the previous formula by taking the inverse approach, with the expression FFV being equivalent to the product of PV, (1 plus i), and n. In this scenario, the cash flow will be divided for each year, resulting in a calculation of (1 i)n, where n represents the duration until the receipt of cash flow. As a consequence of these factors, the outcome manifests as the current value.

It can be tempting to disregard uneven cash flows, however, their presence introduces a level of complexity. As enterprises experience sustained expansion, it is not uncommon for the rate of cash flow growth to decelerate.

In order to compute the present value in cash flows that are not evenly distributed, it is necessary to make an assessment of the cash flow for each year and subsequently apply an appropriate discount. Subsequently, you calculate the collective sum, resulting in the determination of the current value. This prompts the subsequent logical inquiry: Which discount rate ought to be selected? To address this, you may utilize Microsoft Excel or Google Sheets, which will greatly facilitate your present value computations.

Now, you will be required to address the matter of residual value. Occasionally, value-oriented investors may opt to evaluate the worth of stocks by aggregating all forthcoming cash flows, ensuring the application of discounting back to the present moment. This is the methodology employed to determine the intrinsic value of a security. However, how does one determine the intended significance? If we consider the term "all" to encompass an infinite duration, it follows that we make the assumption of a company's perpetual existence. Let us consider an alternative scenario where the term "all" signifies a span of 100 years. In this case, a notable concern arises with regard to the process of discounting, particularly when the growth rates and cash flows exhibit asymmetry over time. It would be advisable to refrain from perusing that considerably disordered and problematic excel spreadsheet.

In order to address this matter, a considerable number of value investors opt to ascribe an ongoing value or residual value to all the cash inflows beyond a span of 10 years. Predicting future discount and growth rates is a challenging task, therefore it is advisable to establish a 10-year time frame limit. This eliminates the need for calculating residual value.

Exercise Prudence in Handling Extensive Quantities

Certainly, substantial figures are desirable in terms of the yield achieved. Logically speaking. Nevertheless, on certain occasions, they may prove to be too remarkable to be deemed authentic. It is imperative to take into account the viability of the price-earnings to growth (PEG) ratios when evaluating the stocks in question.

Assuming your selected company attains $200 million in sales during the current fiscal year. In order to sustain its ongoing growth rate of 30 percent, the company must generate a total revenue of $260 million in the upcoming fiscal year. That's doable. What developments can be anticipated in the forthcoming decade? What steps will your company take to ensure the achievement of this objective? From where does the company source consistent sales that will result in a continual increase of your sales by a margin of 30 percent? Will they commence serving the Martian population? Excellent! What is the total count of Martians present? What is the method by which they transport their products to the planet Mars? Do Martians even exist? Eventually, sustaining such a growth rate will become increasingly challenging. In light of this observation, it is common for value investors to anticipate even more subdued rates in the forthcoming years.

Furthermore, there appears to be a considerable impediment of $20 billion that has a profound impact on numerous enterprises. Once they reach that threshold, a subsequent downturn in growth occurs. Following the attainment of that benchmark, a decrease in growth is observed. Analogously, an identical occurrence takes place when reaching the threshold of $40 billion. These tiers are in place due to the prevalence of market saturation, resulting in a formidable challenge to achieve further sales growth. Additionally, the company's scale could pose considerable challenges in expeditiously undertaking the necessary changes to resume their trajectory of growth. Consequently, subsequent to the completion of a decade, the value investor adopts a significantly more cautious stance regarding their prognostications.

The Value Investor Mindset

Warren Buffett is among the wealthiest individuals globally, despite living a notably humble lifestyle. Over the course of several decades, he has resided in his current residence without any inclination towards accumulating a multitude of luxurious automobiles, nor allocating his funds towards extravagant possessions such as yachts, which are commonly acquired by individuals of significant wealth such as billionaires. Warren Buffett espouses the investment strategy of value stocks, which entails investing in stocks that possess an intrinsic value that diverges from their perceived worth. This investment approach entails significant long-term ramifications, making it one of the foremost strategies for optimizing your investment gains. Additionally, it proves to be a highly challenging task to execute, as it necessitates a profound

113

comprehension of the intricacies of markets and the psychological disposition of fellow investors who pursue immediate profits. Fortunately, through attentive listening to Warren's statements, we can, to some extent, incorporate several notable advantages associated with value investments.

The fundamental principle underlying value investments is that they involve purchasing shares in a company that possesses intrinsic worth exceeding its present market valuation. On the flip side, you can also engage in the practice of short selling a company that you deem to be overvalued. Warren has involved himself in both endeavors, yet he has gained greater recognition for his adeptness in identifying enterprises with high potential for long-term value appreciation. In order to comprehend the impact of market valuation on companies, one only needs to observe the response of the market to news events. As an illustration, back in the year three years prior, when Dell made an announcement regarding a range of fresh computer offerings within their array of products, shareholders eagerly invested in Dell shares. They viewed this as a significant chance to capitalize on a positive shift in investment. Traders such as Warren harbored somewhat greater skepticism towards Dell. They perceived this organization as one that had traded off long-lasting value in favor of immediate benefits. Their product line lacked innovation, as it primarily consisted of a greater variety of products resulting from the customization of essentially the same existing product. Following the collective demonstration of support for Dell stock, investors soon came to the realization that it had been subject to an exaggerated valuation, subsequently resulting in a downturn in its market performance. Profit could have been generated by an investor through engaging in short selling of the stock. However, it is important to note that short selling is a complex and advanced strategy that may not be suitable for novice investors. Alternatively, value trading, with equal likelihood, can yield similar outcomes.

In the midst of the substantial economic downturn, numerous companies experienced a decrease in their market worth, prompting astute investors such as Buffett to adopt a contrarian approach and strategically acquire these undervalued stocks. Among the listed companies are GM, which currently disburses some of the most substantial dividends across all financial markets. For novice investors, it is crucial to direct your attention towards identifying stocks that are currently undervalued in relation to their true worth. This task is not simple to execute, hence we will require some assistance.

Following Warren

Buffett places his investment on the notion that the inherent worth of a stock surpasses its present market value. I am not proficient in the identification of these stocks, however, it is not a necessity for me to do so. I simply need to carefully review the multitude of comments regularly issued by Buffett and allocate my investments accordingly in those commodities. An instance to illustrate this is the fact that my decision to invest in GM stock solely for the purpose of procuring dividends was exclusively influenced by the counsel of renowned investor Warren Buffett. His contemplation regarding the stock market presents valuable insights for identifying prospective investment opportunities. Autonomously discerning these selections necessitates conducting an exhaustive analysis of a company's financial records, thereby ascertaining their underappreciated status in relation to their existing assets. For ordinary investors, this timeframe represents a significant commitment, necessitating specialized expertise. If you choose to solely adhere to the guidance of reputable value investors, such as Buffett or other accomplished individuals in the field, you have the potential to engage in trading akin to that of a seasoned professional in the realm of value investing. These investments have a longer-term horizon, including those that provide dividends on a multiple occasions throughout the year. If you possess the capacity to invest in the value stocks that Buffett endorses, I would strongly advise you to consider doing so. Up until now, he has demonstrated his ability to offer exceptionally valuable counsel, resulting in consistent growth of my returns over the course of several years.

Secondly, incorporate your exchange with a preferred mode of payment.

After making a selection for the exchange, the subsequent task entails assembling your confidential documents. The visuals might comprise photographs of a driver's license and social security number, alongside details pertaining to your organization and the origin of financial resources, contingent upon the specific exchange.

The data that could be required may differ subject to your place of residence and the corresponding applicable regulations. Establishing a traditional brokerage account bears striking resemblance to the procedures involved in establishing a hedge fund.

The payment option will be made accessible to you once the trade has duly authenticated your identification and legal status. The majority of exchanges offer the option to promptly connect your account with a financial institution, or alternatively, you can make use of a debit or credit card to engage in the exchange.

Due to the potential volatility inherent in cryptocurrencies, it is feasible to make a purchase of Bitcoin utilizing a credit card. Nevertheless, it is generally advised against due to the significant level of risk associated with such an approach. Despite the legality of Bit coins in the United States, certain banking institutions are discontented with the concept and may scrutinize, or even decline, depositing funds to websites or exchanges associated with Crypto currency.

It is advisable to administer an examination as a means of verifying that your financial institution effectively transfers/deposits funds into the alternate account you have designated.

Deposits conducted through a financial institution account, a debit card, or a credit card are susceptible to a range of charges. According to the company's statement, Coinbase is considered to be a trustworthy platform suitable for individuals who are new to crypto trading. They offer a fee of 1.49 percent for bank transfers and a fee of 3.99 percent for debit and credit card transactions.

A thorough examination of the fees associated with each fee option is imperative to assist you in determining the most suitable one for your needs and to make an informed selection from the available options.

Exchanges levy additional charges corresponding to the magnitude of the fund transacted. The pricing structure could potentially encompass either a fixed fee (in cases where the level of trading activity is minimal) or a percentage proportionate to the overall value of the transactions conducted. Credit cards are subject to a processing fee that is commensurate with the associated transaction charges.

Proceed with Step Three: Generate a Purchase Order

After meticulously selecting a trading platform and successfully establishing a connection with a verified payment method, you are now eligible to procure Bit coin and various other cryptographic currencies. In recent times, there has been a discernible rise in the popularity of Bit coin exchanges, resulting in increased accessibility for a wider range of individuals. They have experienced substantial growth in both liquidity and the breadth of their expertise.

The procedural modifications implemented at crypto currency exchanges bear resemblance to the notion of a platform for the exchange of digital currencies.

A previously perceived fraudulent or ethically questionable business is undergoing a gradual yet constant transition into a reputable enterprise that has captivated the interest of prominent stakeholders in the market for economic offerings.

Presently, cryptocurrency exchanges have advanced to a stage where they execute operations that are nearly comparable to those conducted by traditional stock brokerage firms.

After choosing an exchange and linking a payment method to your account, you are prepared to commence your voyage. Currently, cryptocurrency exchanges offer a wide range of order types and investment opportunities.

Virtually all cryptocurrency exchanges incorporate both market orders and limit orders, with certain platforms even providing the option for stop-loss orders.

Kraken exhibits the highest level of diversity among the aforementioned exchanges in relation to the variety of order types available.

Kraken1 accepts a variety of order types, including market orders, restriction orders, prevent-loss orders, prevent-restrict orders, take-earnings orders, and take-profit limit orders.

In addition to the abundance of order types available, exchanges now offer mechanisms for establishing recurring investments, thereby allowing customers to engage in dollar cost averaging for their preferred investment options.

As an illustration, on the Coin base platform, individuals have the option to establish recurring transactions on a daily, weekly, or monthly basis, tailoring it to their personal preferences.

Increase Your Earnings

On the other hand, an amplification in earnings presents itself as the counterpart to the act of repaying debts. In regard to the means of attaining wealth, increasing your income can be described as one of the most efficacious measures. Ultimately, there is a limit to how much one can economize within their budget.

There are several avenues through which you can augment your income, such as:

⬜ Gaining new skills

Resuming one's education

⬚ Discussions on remuneration" or "⬚ Compensation talks

Utilizing the available working hours from 9-5

Supplementary employment or additional source of income.

Establishing sources of residual revenue

I would recommend leveraging your current employment to augment your earnings. Are there any available opportunities for professional development or supplemental overtime that would provide additional compensation? Does your place of employment offer any financial assistance for tuition purposes? Is there potential for career progression into higher remunerative roles?

After maximizing the financial potential of your current occupation, proceed to investigate alternative approaches for augmenting your earnings.

For the majority of individuals, engaging in a side hustle is the most straightforward and accessible avenue to commence augmenting your financial resources. Supplementary income endeavors can encompass anything from engaging in part-time employment to establishing a secondary enterprise of considerable complexity.

No matter which options for augmenting your earnings are most accessible, it is crucial to be aware that generating additional income is a fundamental aspect of building wealth.

7. Make an investment

To amass wealth, it is imperative to allocate investments towards debt payment while simultaneously augmenting one's income.

Investment plays a pivotal role in attaining wealth as it empowers individuals to generate passive income without active labor. In alternative terms, investing can serve as a method by which individuals can utilize their funds to generate returns, thereby enabling them to accumulate wealth without needing to allocate additional time towards employment for the purpose of earning additional income.

Let us advance the discussion. Conventional occupations necessitate the exchange of time and exertion in order to obtain financial remuneration. You allocate funds into an investment vehicle, and passively witness the growth of your capital over an extended period without any active involvement on your part. By engaging in long-term investment, one can harness the power of compound interest, thereby realizing gains from the accumulated interest on their assets.

The ability to generate wealth without trading your time and labor is an essential element in effective wealth accumulation. There exists no alternative method that provides a predictable outcome of generating an equivalent sum of income within a comparable timeframe, unless one experiences significant success on par with a company like Amazon in the future.

Nevertheless, not all investments hold identical weight, and there are inherent risks entailed. To offset these risks, it is advisable to pursue diversification and adopt a far-sighted perspective.

Furthermore, it is not imperative to possess extensive expertise in selecting stocks in order to generate financial gains. Index funds and target-date funds are highly effective options for achieving portfolio diversification with minimal effort, as they allow you to invest in a wide market rather than individual companies. Target date funds also undergo automatic adjustments to reduce risk as the target date draws near.

Furthermore, it is advised to seek out online sources such as blogs, podcasts, and assorted resources that can facilitate your understanding of various investment options, enabling you to commence the investment process promptly. In terms of the return on investment one achieves over the course of their investing journey, the passage of time spent actively participating in the market is of utmost importance.

Although individual circumstances may vary, it is generally more advantageous to initiate retirement planning by considering options such as a 401(k), owing to their tax incentivized nature and potential supplementary benefits, such as employer contribution match. Individual retirement accounts (IRAs) are a highly advantageous investment instrument that is open for participation irrespective of one's employment situation.

Once you have laid the groundwork for your core retirement investments, it may be prudent to explore the acquisition of alternative assets, such as real estate, REITs (real estate investment trusts), cryptocurrency, or other viable options.

Prominence In Quality No Longer Holds Priority

Many individuals hold the belief that the most effective approach to preserving the quality of one's property is through personal involvement in all maintenance tasks. I do not disagree with this notion; however, when one starts to view things from this perspective, one inevitably teeters on the brink of fostering an emotional bond with one's belongings. You should have never

Enthusiastic contribution to your entrepreneurial assets. I acknowledge that this task presents a significant challenge, as I have occasionally been responsible for it in a genuine manner.

Not all properties should be maintained at the same standards as you would your own residence. If you happen to be engaged in the rental of high-end properties, perhaps. However, the majority of rental properties do not possess the same level of quality. In the past, I have encountered situations where I have dealt with properties in remote areas that were not conducive to attracting high-quality occupants. Therefore, it would have been unnecessary and extravagant to furnish such properties with premium materials. You would not be able to increase the rental price for the property anyway, as market values impose certain limits on how high you can go. Thus, it appears acceptable to align the quality of materials with both the property's location and the quality of tenants. While I do not wish to condone slumlording in any way, it does not seem logical or reasonable to expect C or B-grade properties to be maintained at the same level of quality as A-grade properties.

I know myself. If I were to become the owner of the investment properties, I would maintain a discerning approach in ensuring that they meet the high standards to which I am accustomed. Consequently, I would maintain the highest quality standards for all my properties, regardless of the practicality of such an approach. By entrusting the oversight of the property to a qualified supervisor, I am freed from concerns regarding the property's maintenance and adherence to high standards, as I do not need to personally inspect the properties. The properties are currently maintained in excellent condition; however, I am not concerned about distinguishing between rental-grade carpeting and luxury-grade carpeting, as I believe both options are satisfactory.

What is the level of time commitment and emotional well-being required to maintain a property in accordance with your desired standards? Now, consider the comparative level of compensation that would be received for undertaking such a task. In my personal perspective, although I would greatly appreciate having all of my properties in their optimal condition, the level of dedication and effort required to achieve such a standard does not justify my concern. Furthermore, it is far from being a singular endeavor. While achieving such a high standard is a significant achievement, the subsequent task is to consistently sustain them at that level.

Enlisting the services of a property supervisor relieves me from the need to vigilantly monitor and scrutinize the state of my properties from a distant and detached perspective. While numerous individuals might find themselves descending into despair upon the realization that they cannot lay eyes upon their belongings or witness the precise state they are in, I, on the other hand, find solace in this arrangement as it alleviates my burdens and diminishes the level of stress I experience.

You will be required to place trust in other individuals.

When delegating tasks to others, it is imperative to have confidence in their abilities. The lower the amount of work you undertake, the greater the workload imposed on others to complete tasks on your behalf, which in turn necessitates a greater number of individuals whom you must rely upon. Many individuals lack trust in others and struggle to establish trust with them. If you anticipate relinquishing your trust in others to handle your assets or manage your affairs, then be prepared to personally oversee these matters.

For those individuals among us who are inclined to place their trust in others, it is unrealistic to anticipate a perpetually flawless outcome or to assume that those we currently rely on will never betray our trust in the future. Occurrences transpire, necessitating the evaluation of the advantages and disadvantages of entrusting others with the fulfillment of one's obligations, understanding that there is a possibility of occasional wavering or betrayal, while alternatively shouldering the burden entirely on one's own. On a few occasions, I have encountered challenging circumstances resulting from my reliance on others. That is a fact you must face. However, I would still opt for experiencing some setbacks rather than undertaking all the labor myself, as it would alleviate the inconvenience.

Adopt an Entrepreneurial Perspective

This instigates a broader concept, namely commerce. Let us consider the scenario where you commence a business venture. You have demonstrated exceptional skill in crafting exquisite pizzas, thereby compelling numerous individuals to strongly advocate for the establishment of your own pizza business. There are two options available for determining the approach this business adopts in relation to the foundational establishment.

Option one: You are the crucial individual responsible for the creation of the pizzas. Should you choose to take a leave of absence, the production of pizzas will be put on hold. By employing this approach, you will not receive any compensation. Your physical presence significantly influences the financial results.

Alternative: "Alternative option: Develop comprehensive frameworks and methodologies for your pizza establishment, enabling anyone to replicate the unique pizza recipes and techniques devised by your organization." Through this action, you can remove yourself from the situation and furthermore...

Delegates acting on your behalf. When individuals go on vacation, sales remain unaffected. This process largely constitutes the operational framework of establishments. The original inventors of pizza and the initial preparers of hamburgers are not essential for the execution of the required tasks in order to obtain financial remuneration.

The methods of operating a pizza business and engaging in real estate investments can be largely viewed as synonymous in terms of two approaches: conducting all the necessary tasks personally or delegating them to others. Kindly disclose the course of action you have chosen for enhancing your land investments, as it aligns with the previous deliberations focused on strengthening your assets and adhering to your natural tendencies. In case you're

Given the apparent bias, it might be prudent for you to personally undertake the task instead. If you possess a broader perspective and prioritize the overall objective, it may be more advisable to manage a team of individuals to effectively accomplish the tasks at hand.

This notion can be utilized in two manners: determining the foundational framework one must pursue, and deliberating on the manner in which one should shape their selection of strategy. For undertaking any specialized task, it would be advisable to initially select a collaborative platform that is less inclined towards technical intricacies. If you possess expertise in more specialized tasks, you may select a system tailored to those specific requirements. However, it is important to note that you also have the option, in due course, to reconfigure the same process in a manner that facilitates a transition from the technical side to a more strategic perspective.

In his published works, Robert Kiyosaki offers extensive clarification regarding the differentiation between being an entrepreneur and an employee. The differentiation between those two employment positions lies in the practice of reallocating tasks or resources. When you agree to delegate certain aspects of the business, by hiring someone else to handle them, you commence to emancipate yourself from personally undertaking all the decision-making and operational tasks. This entails adopting an entrepreneurial approach, wherein one strives to become an entrepreneur instead of succumbing to the role of an employee carrying out all the tasks.

Methods For Establishing Your Investment Strategy

Possessing an investment strategy is an essential component of achieving success in the realm of stock market trading. Devoid of it, you are essentially navigating blindly. Although your proficiency in technical analysis is admirable, you may encounter difficulty in establishing a definitive trajectory for your portfolio. Certainly, it is still feasible for you to generate income. Nonetheless, you will not achieve the optimal return on your investment.

It is imperative for you to establish a strategic course of action. Once you have formulated this plan, you may proceed with identifying the stocks that align with your objectives. In the following chapter, we will examine three highly effective investment strategies that can result in substantial financial gains.

Buy and Hold

The "buy and hold" approach epitomizes a strategy focused on long-term investment. In this particular strategy, one would acquire assets and retain ownership of them until their value experiences a significant increase. Upon reaching that juncture, you have the opportunity to divest your holdings. It is important to acknowledge that the term "long term" in stock trading refers to any period of time exceeding one month. Therefore, it is reasonable to anticipate maintaining ownership of stocks for a minimum duration of one month.

This approach proves to be highly effective in identifying stocks that are currently undervalued. As an illustration, consider the organizations that possess commendable past performances but have encountered challenging circumstances. Oil companies exemplify this phenomenon. Oil companies bear no responsibility for geopolitical factors that contribute to the decline in oil prices. However, in instances where the cost of oil drastically decreases, oil corporations experience significant adverse impacts.

In order to take advantage of this phenomenon, one may choose to acquire oil stocks at a time of decline. Subsequently, you retain possession of them until such time as the price of oil experiences a recovery. Consequently, there is a resurgence in oil stocks. In certain instances, it could potentially be a matter of a few days. Alternatively, in different circumstances, it could pertain to a matter of several weeks. In essence, it is imperative that you remain well-informed about current events and advancements spanning multiple industries.

High-Frequency Trading

High-frequency trading, alternatively referred to as HFT, constitutes an integral practice among individuals engaged in day trading. This approach is a strategy with a limited duration. It encompasses the repetitive execution of numerous trading transactions. This strategy does not yield substantial financial gains per trade. Nevertheless, as you compound your gains across a substantial number of transactions, the resultant profits accumulate.

In order to effectively execute this methodology, it is imperative to identify a stock that is being traded within a specified range. This implies that they ascend to a predetermined level before descending to a designated threshold. Conversely, they generally adhere to these boundaries. Consequently, one can reasonably anticipate the trajectory of the price movement.

Frequently, high-frequency traders generate minimal profits per individual transaction. However, upon calculating the aggregate number of transactions, the outcomes may accumulate to a sum of hundreds of dollars per day. Consequently, employing this approach can be deemed as a prudent strategy when implementing the "buy and hold" tactic with alternative stocks.

Additionally, high-frequency trading proves to be advantageous for investors commencing their endeavors with limited initial investment capital. Therefore, high-frequency traders repeatedly transfer the same pool of investment capital. For example, repeatedly investing $1,000 and consistently generating profits on the initial investment. Ultimately, they yield profits equivalent to a $100,000 investment.

As an inexperienced investor, it is advisable for you to take High-Frequency Trading (HFT) into consideration. It will necessitate a portion of your time being dedicated to configuring transactions on your computer. However, once you acquire proficiency, it becomes effortless to arrange all the necessary elements at the commencement of your day, and subsequently relax while observing the ensuing events.

Value Investing

Value investing encompasses the strategy of identifying stocks that are currently undervalued and retaining them in one's portfolio until they experience a favorable recovery. Accordingly, the primary distinction between value investing and the buy and hold strategy lies in the fact that value investing aims to identify companies poised for a prompt rebound. In the context of the buy and hold strategy, the objective is to retain ownership of stocks for a period exceeding one month. Within the framework of value investing, the objective is to retain ownership of stocks over a period of several days or a few weeks.

The key to successful value investing lies in identifying stocks that are positioned to experience a prompt rebound. In order to implement the value investing strategy, it is necessary to conduct an analysis of a company's book value. The expression "book value" pertains to the valuation of a company's shares derived from its financial records. Consequently, an organization's financial statements will provide insight into the true value of their stock price. Subsequently, it is imperative to conduct a comparative analysis between the company's book value and its market valuation. In the event that the market valuation of the company falls short of its book value, it can be concluded that the company is undervalued.

Nevertheless, there is an underlying caveat.

When engaging in value investing, it is imperative to ascertain that the company does not find itself in a precarious situation. Consequently, it is imperative that you conduct your homework with meticulousness. In certain instances, a corporation might be undergoing a transitory circumstance. This does not indicate inadequate administration or unfavorable financial conditions. Therefore, one can anticipate a recovery from the company.

In the realm of value investing, events have the potential to transpire with remarkable swiftness. Therefore, it is imperative for you to be adequately prepared for any potential alterations that may occur. However, this approach serves as a highly effective strategy in bridging the gap between long-term investment and high-frequency trading.

www.ingramcontent.com/pod-product-compliance
Lightning Source LLC
Chambersburg PA
CBHW071654210326
41597CB00017B/2201